PIONEER VALLEY E

MONARCH JOURNEY

MICHÈLE DUFRESNE

TABLE OF CONTENTS

Did you know that millions of monarch butterflies travel across the world each year? Every fall before the weather turns too cold, monarch butterflies **migrate** south. They may travel as many as 3,000 miles to find a warm place like California or Mexico.

Monarch Butterfly
MIGRATION

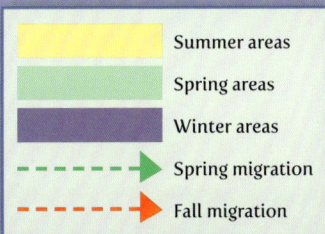

SUMMER

SUMMER

SPRING

WINTER

WINTER

▨ Summer areas	
▨ Spring areas	
▨ Winter areas	
- - - ➤	Spring migration
- - - ➤	Fall migration

The monarch butterfly is the only butterfly that migrates. They cannot survive in the cold. To protect themselves, they move to a warm place every winter.

Even though monarch butterflies only make this long journey once in their lifetime, they somehow know exactly where to go. They fly along the same route as their parents and grandparents. They even rest in the same spots.

Some scientists believe that monarch butterflies know where to travel by feeling the earth's magnetic field and watching the position of the sun. Others believe that butterflies who flew before them left behind a scent to follow.

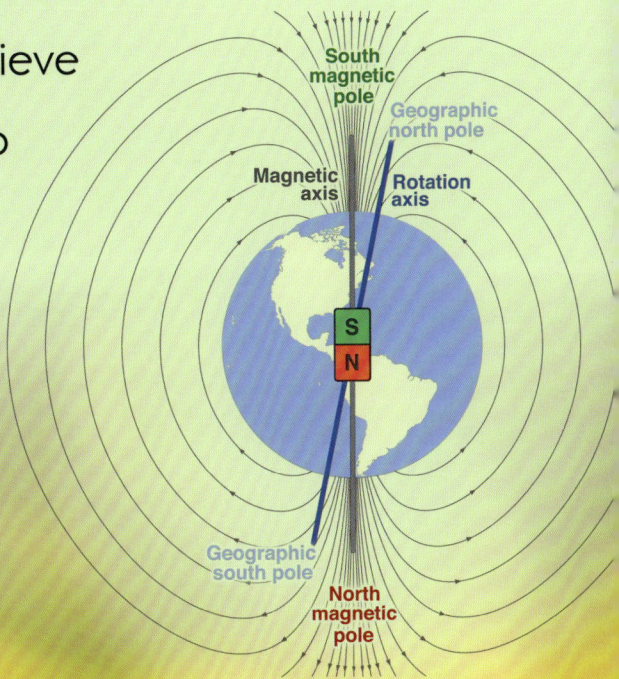

South magnetic pole

Geographic north pole

Magnetic axis

Rotation axis

S

N

Geographic south pole

North magnetic pole

Earth is a very big magnet. The North and South Poles are where the magnet is strongest. The area around the poles is known as the magnetic field.

How can a small butterfly make such a long trip? The monarch butterfly stores fat in its body. This fat is used as fuel to help it make the long trip south. It lasts until the butterfly flies back north in the spring.

As the monarch flies south, it stops along the way to sip nectar from flowers and plants. Some scientists think that the butterflies may save their fuel by gliding on air currents as they make the long trip south.

During their migration, monarch butterflies cluster together in tight groups. The butterflies in the center are kept safe from bad weather and predators. They take turns hiding in the middle of the group.

➤ Monarch butterflies can travel 50 to 100 miles each day. It can take them up to two months to make their long journey south.

Male monarch butterflies usually die after migrating south in the winter. Only the female butterflies survive to make the journey back. As the female butterflies head north, they lay tiny, round eggs on milkweed plants along the way. They die soon after that.

➤ Some monarch butterflies have an average life span of only 2 to 6 weeks.

In a few days, small yellow-and-white striped caterpillars hatch from the eggs. For the first two weeks of their lives, these tiny caterpillars eat constantly. They feed on milkweed leaves and shed their skin as they grow.

After two weeks, the caterpillars **transform** into pupae. They put their heads down and attach to a leaf or twig. Then they shed their skin one last time. The skin becomes a hard layer called a chrysalis. The chrysalis starts out bright green and slowly turns white, then clear.

pupa

chrysalis

After another two weeks,
the caterpillars come out of
the chrysalis, but they are no longer
caterpillars—they are butterflies!

➤ This change from caterpillar to
butterfly is called a **metamorphosis**.

The monarch butterfly has bright orange wings with black lines and white spots. Like other colorful animals, the monarch butterfly's wings tell predators that it is poisonous.

The milkweed that the monarch caterpillar eats has poisonous **toxins**. The caterpillar stores the toxins in its body. The toxins make the monarch butterfly taste bitter. Once a bird tastes a monarch butterfly, it will learn to stay away.

➤ Viceroy butterflies are not poisonous or bitter, but they look a lot like monarch butterflies. Predators stay away from viceroy butterflies because of their bright orange wings.

Viceroy butterflies have a line on their lower wings.

Scientists believe that monarch butterflies have been making their amazing journey for thousands of years. But monarch butterflies are in danger now. Their numbers are decreasing.

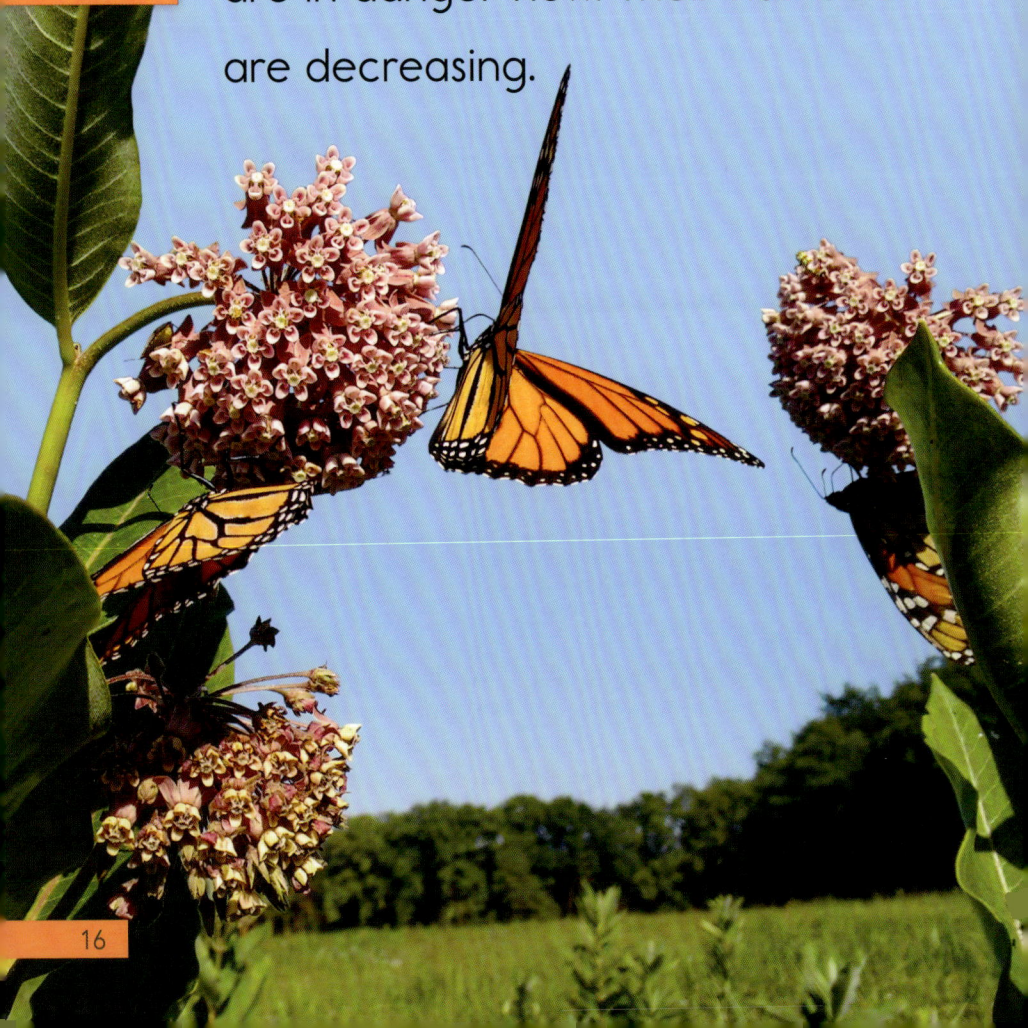

The biggest danger to monarch butterflies is people. Some people do not like milkweed, and they mow it down or spray it with **pesticides**. They do not understand how important milkweed is to the monarch butterfly.

When we cut down trees in the forest to make wood, we may be cutting down the homes and rest stops where monarch butterflies have stayed for thousands of years.

Climate change is affecting these beautiful butterflies too. Sudden changes in temperature and extreme weather such as high winds and rain can be harmful to monarch butterflies.

➤ Monarch butterflies cannot fly if their body temperature is lower than 86 degrees. They sometimes sit in sunny areas to warm up.

It is important to save these insects. We need monarch butterflies because they help to pollinate plants.

You can help monarch butterflies. Try not to use pesticides in your gardens. If you have milkweed in your yard, let a little bit of it grow. Butterflies will lay their eggs on it, and caterpillars will eat it. You can also help by planting flowers with nectar for butterflies to drink.

GLOSSARY

metamorphosis: changing from one creature into another

migrate: to move from one area to another

pesticides: chemicals that kill anything that might damage a plant or crop

toxins: poisonous substances produced by a living thing

transform: to completely change

INDEX